a Host of Angels

Treasures of the Vatican Library
(Book Illustration)

a Host of Angels

Turner Publishing, Inc.

ATLANTA

The illustrations in this book are taken from Latin volumes in the collections of the
Vatican Library, including the Barberini, Capponi, Chigi, Borghese, Ottoboni, and
Rossiano collections. The sources for each illustration appear on page 80.

Published by Turner Publishing, Inc.
A Subsidiary of Turner Broadcasting System, Inc.
1050 Techwood Drive, N.W.
Atlanta, Georgia 30318

First Edition 10 9 8 7 6 5 4 3 2 1
ISBN: 1-57036-100-2

Printed in the U.S.A.

Treasures of the Vatican Library:
Book Illustration

A HOST OF ANGELS, a small volume in the Treasures of the Vatican Library series, offers a selection of miniature masterworks of book illustration from the collections of one of the world's greatest repositories of classical, medieval, and Renaissance culture. The Vatican Library, for six hundred years celebrated as a center of learning and a monument to the art of the book, is, nevertheless, little known to the general public, for admission to the library traditionally has been restricted to qualified scholars. Since very few outside the scholarly community have ever been privileged to examine the magnificent hand-lettered and illuminated manuscript books in the library's collections, the artwork selected for the series volumes is all the more poignant, fascinating, and appealing.

Of course, the popes had always maintained a library, but in the fifteenth century, Pope Nicholas V decided to build an edifice of unrivaled magnificence to house the papacy's growing collections—to serve the entire "court of Rome," the clerics and scholars associated with the papal palace. Pope Sixtus IV added to what Nicholas had begun, providing the library with a suite of beautifully frescoed rooms and furnishing it with heavy wooden benches, to which the precious works were actually chained. But, most significantly, like the popes who succeeded him, Sixtus added books. By 1455 the library held 1,200 volumes, and a catalogue compiled in 1481 listed 3,500, making it by far the largest collection of books in the Western world.

And the Vatican Library has kept growing: through purchase, commission, donation, and military conquest. Nor did the popes restrict themselves to ecclesiastical subjects. Bibles, theological texts, and commentaries on canon law are here in abundance, to be sure, but so are the Latin and Greek classics that placed the Vatican Library at the very heart of all Renaissance learning. Over the centuries, the library has acquired some of world's most significant collections of literary works, including the Palatine Library of Heidelberg, the Cerulli collection of Persian and Ethiopian manuscripts, the great Renaissance libraries of the Duke of Urbino and of Queen Christiana of Sweden, and the matchless seventeenth-century collections of the Barberini, the Ottoboni, and Chigi. Today the library contains over one million printed books—including eight thousand published during the first fifty years of the printing press—in addition to 150,000 manuscripts and some 100,000 prints. Assiduously collected and carefully preserved over the course of almost six hundred years, these unique works of art and knowledge, ranging from the secular to the profane, are featured in this ongoing series, Treasures of the Vatican Library, for the delectation of lovers of great books and breathtaking works of art.

Are not all angels spirits
in the divine service, sent to
serve for the sake of those who
are to inherit salvation?

HEBREWS 1:14

Bless the Lord, O you his angels,

you mighty ones who do his

bidding, obedient to his

spoken word.

Bless the Lord, all his hosts,

his ministers that do his will.

PSALMS 103:20–21

Then I looked, and I heard
the voice of many angels
surrounding the throne and the
living creatures and the elders;
they numbered myriads of
myriads and thousands
of thousands . . .

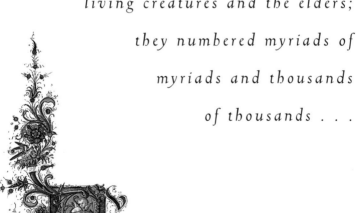

REVELATIONS 5:11

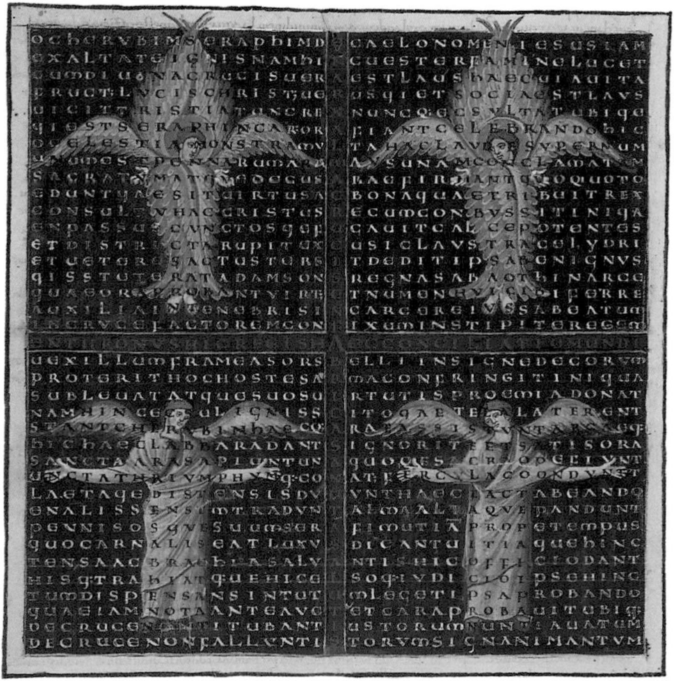

Top left panel:

```
OCHERUBIMSERAPHIMD
EXALTATEIGNISNAMBI
GUMDIUSNACRUISUERA
ERUCTLUCISCHRISTUG
UICITTRISTIATUNCRE
UISSTSGRAPHINCAFOR
OELESTIAMONSTRAQUI
MAUOGSTDONARRUGA
SACRAMMAUITGEOGUS
GDUNTIIAESITUIRTUSA
CONSULUNHAECRISTUS
ENPASSUSCUNCTOSQP
ETDISTRICTURAPIUIX
ETUETORSACTOSTORS
QISSTUTERATADAMSON
MAUOGSGOROANTUITE
AUXILIAINUONERISI
GCRUCELACTOREMCON
```

Top right panel:

```
CAGLONOMENIESUSLAM
CUESTGREAMINCLOGET
ETSLAUSHAECUIAUITA
USQETSOCIACSTLAUS
NUNCQGCSUITATUBIQ
FIANTCELEBRANDOBIC
TAHAECLAUDASUPERNUM
ASUNAMCOSLAMATA
RAGFIRMANTQUOQUOTO
BONAQUAETRIBUITREX
ECUMCONBUSSITINIQA
GAUITCALCEPOTENTOS
USICLAUSTRACELYDRI
TDEDITIPSAORNIGNUS
REGNASABAOTHINARCO
TNUMONYSNIIFERRE
CARCORGISSABEATUQ
IXUMINSTIPITERECO
```

Bottom left panel:

```
UEXILLUMFRAMEASORS
PROTEGRITHOCHOSTESA
SUBLEUATATQUESUOSU
NAMHINCGOSULIGNISS
STANTUICHERUBINHAECCO
BICHAECLABRARADANT
SANCTAIRSSADIUNTUN
UECTATIRIUMPHUSGCO
LAGTAGEDISTENSISDU
ONALISSENSUMTRADUN
PENNISOSQUSUGMSGR
QUOCARNALICEATLUX
TONSAACBRACHIASALU
HISGTRAHATQUEHICG
TUMDISPENSANSINTOT
QUASIAMNOTAANTEAUG
OGCROGCUITUBANT
DECRUCENONFALLUNTI
```

Bottom right panel:

```
ELLIINSIGNEDECORUO
MACONERINGITINIQUA
RTUTISPROGMIADONAT
ITOGAETEALATERGNT
RAMESSSIATLATERONS
SIGNORITTGSTISORA
QUOGCSCROOGELUNT
ATFIRCGLAGOONDUNT
UNTHAGCTACTABGANDO
ALUMALTAQUEPANDUNT
FIMUTIAPROPGTEMPUS
DICANTUTIAQUEHINC
NTISHICOFFICLODANT
SOGIUDICIOPSGHING
OLOGETIIPSAPROBANDO
ETGARAPROBAUITQHUG
USTORUMQUNTIAUATUM
TORUMSIGNANIMANTUM
```

Then the man said,

"This at last is bone of my

bones and flesh of my flesh;

this one shall be called Woman,

for out of Man this one

was taken."

GENESIS 1:27

Then Abraham reached out his hand

and took the knife to kill his son.

But the angel of the Lord called to

him from heaven, and said,

"Abraham, Abraham!" And he said,

"Here I am." He said, "Do not lay

your hand on the boy or do anything

to him; for now I know that you fear

God, since you have not withheld

your son, your only son, from me."

GENESIS 22:10–12

VERBA · HIEREMIE · FILII · ELCHIE

Then the Lord put out his hand

and touched my mouth;

and the Lord said to me,

"Now I have put my

words in your mouth. . . ."

JEREMIAH 1:9

" . . . Say no more! Do not fear for them, my sister. For a good angel will accompany him; his journey will be successful, and he will come back in good health."

TOBIT 5:21-22

+ TOBIAS EX CIVITATE ET TRIBV +

"Truly I tell you, among those born of women no one has arisen greater than John the Baptist; yet the least in the kingdom of heaven is greater than he."

MATTHEW 11:11

In the sixth month the angel
Gabriel was sent by God to a town
in Galilee called Nazareth. . . .

. . . to a virgin engaged to a man whose name was Joseph, of the house of David.

The virgin's name was Mary.

And he came to her and said,

"Greetings, favored one!

The Lord is with you."

LUKE 1:27–28

AVE GRATIA PLENA
DOMINVS TECVM

But she was much perplexed by his words and pondered what sort of greeting this might be. The angel said to her, "Do not be afraid, Mary, for you have found favor with God. And now, you will conceive in your womb and bear a son, and you will name him Jesus."

LUKE 1:29–31

Mary said to the angel,
"How can this be,
since I am a virgin?"
The angel said to her,
"The Holy Spirit will
come upon you, and the
power of the Most High
will overshadow you. . . ."

LUKE 1:34–35

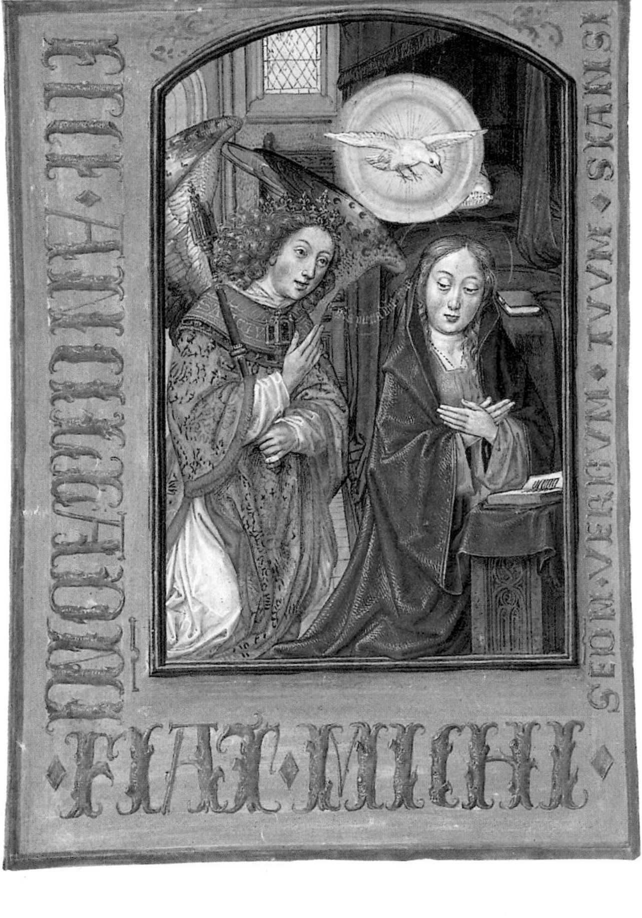
FIAT MICHI

. . . therefore the child

to be born will be holy;

he will be called Son of God.

LUKE 1:35

Then Mary said,

"Here am I, the servant

of the Lord; let it be with me

according to your word."

Then the angel departed from her.

In that region there were
shepherds living in the fields,
keeping watch over their
flock by night.
Then an angel of the Lord stood
before them, and the glory of the
Lord shone around them,
and they were terrified.

LUKE 2:8-9

But the angel said to them,

"Do not be afraid; for see—

I am bringing you good news of

great joy for all the people . . . "

LUKE 2:10

. . . to you is born this day in
the city of David a Savior,
who is the Messiah, the Lord.

LUKE 2:11

And suddenly there was
with the angel a multitude
of the heavenly host,
praising God and saying,
"Glory to God in the
highest heaven, and on earth
peace among those
whom he favors!"

LUKE 2:13–14

And she gave birth to her firstborn son and wrapped him in bands of cloth, and laid him in a manger, because there was no place for them in the inn.

LUKE 2:7

"This will be a sign for you:
you will find a child wrapped
in bands of cloth and
lying in a manger."

LUKE 2:12

. . . and he was called Jesus,

the name given by the angel . . .

LUKE 2:21

He was in the wilderness

forty days, tempted by Satan;

and he was with the wild beasts;

and the angels waited on him.

PAVLVS

PAVLVS SERVVS IESV CRISTI

Now as he was going along
and approaching Damascus,
suddenly a light from heaven
flashed around him.
He fell to the ground and heard
a voice saying to him, "Saul,
Saul, why do you persecute me?"
He asked, "Who are you, Lord?"
The reply came, "I am Jesus. . . ."

ACTS 9:3–7

"Henceforth all generations

will call me blessed."

LUKE 1:48

Then Jesus, crying with
a loud voice, said,
"Father, into your hands
I commend my spirit."
Having said this
he breathed his last.

LUKE 23:46

After the sabbath, as the first day

of the week was dawning,

Mary Magdalene and the other

Mary went to see the tomb.

And suddenly there was a great

earthquake; for an angel of the Lord,

descending from heaven, came and

rolled back the stone and sat on it.

MATTHEW 28:1–2

His appearance was like lightning,
and his clothing white as snow.
For fear of him the guards shook
and became like dead men.
But the angel said to the women,
"Do not be afraid; I know that
you are looking for Jesus who was
crucified. He is not here; for he
has been raised, as he said.
Come, see the place where he lay."

MATTHEW 28:3–6

". . . And remember,

I am with you always,

to the end of the age."

MATTHEW 28:20

"When the Son of Man comes in his glory, and all the angels with him, then he will sit on the throne of his glory."

MATTHEW 25:31

The revelation of Jesus Christ . . .
he made it known by sending his
angel to his servant John, who
testified to the word of God. . . .

REVELATIONS 1:1

APOCALIPSIS · IESV · CHRISTI

Praise the Lord! Praise the
Lord from the heavens;
praise him in the heights!
Praise him, all his angels;
praise him, all his host!
Praise him, sun and moon;
praise him, all you
shining stars!

PSALMS 148:1–3

Blessed is the one who reads

aloud the words of the prophecy,

and blessed are those who

hear and who keep what

is written in it. . . .

REVELATIONS 1:3

Make a Joyful noise

to God, all the earth;

sing the glory of his name. . . .

PSALMS 66: 1–2

". . . What are human beings
that you are mindful of them, or
mortals, that you care for them?
You have made them for a little
while lower than the angels;
you have crowned them with
glory and honor. . . ."

Hebrews 2:6–7

For he will command his angels
concerning you to guard you
in all your ways.
On their hands they will bear
you up, so that you will not
dash your foot against a stone.
You will tread on the lion
and the adder, the young lion
and the serpent you will
trample under foot.

PSALMS 91:11-13

Cover, half-title page, and frontispiece: Latin volume 3769 in the Vatican Library Collection; p. 7: Latin volume 3769 in the Vatican Library Collection; p. 9: Latin volume CIV 109 in the Chigi Collection; p. 10: Latin volume 76 in the Barberini Collection; p. 13: Latin Volume 124 in the Rossiano Collection; p. 14: Latin volume 183 in the Borghese Collection; p. 17: Latin volume CVII 205 in the Chigi Collection; p. 18: Latin volume 2 in the Urbino Collection; p. 21: Latin volume 213 in the Urbino Collection; pp. 22-24: Latin volume 610 in the Barberini Collection; p. 25: Latin volume 487 in the Barberini Collection; Latin volume 3781 in the Vatican Library Collection; p. 29: Latin volume C VIII 234 in the Chigi Collection; p. 30: Latin volume C VIII 230 in the Chigi Collection; p. 33: Latin volume 3770 in the Vatican Library Collection; p. 34: Latin volume 183 in the Borghese Collection; p. 37: Latin volume C IV 111 in the Chigi Collection; p. 38: Latin volume 3770 in the Vatican Library Collection; p. 41: Latin volume 218 in the Capponi Collection; p. 42: Latin volume 487 in the Barberini Collection; p. 45: Latin volume 183 in the Borghese Collection; p. 46: Latin volume 381 in the Barberini Collection; p. 48: Latin volume 2 in the Urbino Collection; p. 49: Latin volume 3770 in the Vatican Library Collection; p. 50: Latin volume C IV 109 in the Chigi Collection; p. 53: Latin volume 112 in the Urbino Collection; p. 54: Latin volume 2 in the Urbino Collection; p. 56: Latin volume C IV 109 in the Chigi Collection; p. 57: Latin volume 183 in the Borghese Collection; p. 58: Latin volume 425 in the Barberini Collection; pp. 60-61: Latin volume 610 in the Barberini Collection; p. 62: Latin volume 3805 in the Vatican Library Collection; p. 65: Latin volume C IV 109 in the Chigi Collection; p. 66: Latin volume 3770 in the Vatican Library Collection; p. 68: Latin volume 613 in the Baberini Collection; p. 69 (both images): Latin volume 2 in the Urbino Collection; p. 70: Latin volume 93 in the Urbino Collection; p. 73: Latin volume 124 in the Rossiano Collection; p. 74: Latin volume 585 in the Barberini Collection; p. 77: Latin volume 1 in the Urbino Collection; p. 78: Latin volume 276 in the Urbino Collection. Ornamental illumination on pp. 11, 12, 15, 19, 20, 27, 28, 31, 32, 35, 36, 39, 40, 43, 44, 47, 52, 55, 59, 63, 64, 66, 71, 72, 74, 76, and 78 is from Latin volume 425 in the Urbino Collection.